Rugby Union: Captaincy

Roger Uttley, England captain, in action

Rugby Union: Captaincy

DAVID FROST

WITH ROGER UTTLEY

PELHAM BOOKS

First published in Great Britain by
Pelham Books Ltd
44 Bedford Square
London WC1B 3DU
1981

The illustrations are by Colorsport

ISBN 0 7207 1301 3

Typeset in Great Britain by
Cambrian Typesetters, Farnborough, Hants
and printed and bound in Singapore

Contents

PREFACE

You have only to think of the influence Graham Mourie had on the All Blacks during their three visits to Britain in 1978, 1979 and 1980 to appreciate the importance of captaincy in rugby. At all levels of the game the captain plays a vital role.

Ideally a captain needs to be a natural leader and also to possess a wide knowledge and experience of the game. Many boys and young men are called upon to act as captains before they have had an opportunity to gain much knowledge or experience. This book is intended to help those who are appointed captains to acquire the indispensable knowledge and to understand all the many different aspects of captaincy, both on and off the field.

DAVID FROST
November 1980

1 Qualities

A captain in rugby is more important to the success of his side than a captain in many other sports because of the complexity of the game. The coach may decide on certain tactics before a game, and the captain may have every intention of carrying out those tactics, but, once on the field, the captain may appreciate that the tactics of his coach are not working out. It is then the duty of the captain to evaluate the situation and to direct his team towards different tactics.

One of the charms of rugby is the diversity of tactics available to coach and captain. In the nineteenth century it was common for the ball to be almost entirely confined to the forwards who would try to batter and barge their way ahead. Gradually the game evolved so that the rest of the team, the backs, were brought into play until, in time, it became customary to look upon the forwards as the men who procured the ball for the backs, the faster runners, to attack with. Nowadays, teams will attack through their forwards or through their backs according to the relative strengths of themselves and their opponents.

At one time it was considered that most of the attacking should be done through orthodox passing, or through orthodox passing mixed with unexpected variations of passing. But in the 1930s it became fashionable for teams to use punting by their stand-off halves as the main method of attack. In those days, and for a long time afterwards, it was possible for anyone to punt the ball directly over the touchline and so to make progress towards the opposing goal-line. Now it is not permissible to punt the ball directly over the touchline except from within one's own twenty-five; but punting has been established as a basic tactic.

Punting has often been condemned as a last resort of those who lack the confidence to initiate running and passing. But a good captain will know that there are times in many games when kicking, rather than passing, is likely to prove profitable. The captain must observe the play of his team's opponents and, knowing the resources of his own side, must decide — perhaps making several different decisions in the course of a match — how best to discomfit the enemy and ensure victory for his own team.

It is clear, therefore, that a captain must possess the qualities of intelligence (in a football sense) and of courage to carry out the tactics which his intelligence tells him are needed. This is a rarer combination than might be supposed. There are plenty of men, especially in rugby, who have boundless courage but who lack the footballing vision and intelligence to perceive and appreciate the course a game is taking. There are others, probably fewer in number, who can see what needs to be done to ensure success but who have not the nerve to switch tactics in mid-stream.

It is difficult to think of any sport, except perhaps cricket, in which a captain has so many options to consider as he has in rugby. Mike Brearley has been an outstanding cricket captain because he possesses in abundance the qualities of intelligence and courage. He can see how a battle is progressing and has the guts to make instant decisions for the benefit of his team. In the same way a rugby captain must have his eyes open all the time to assess what is happening, and he must be capable of making a quick decision on how to derive the utmost profit from a particular situation or how to prevent the opposition from exploiting a weakness they may have discovered in his side.

It is very important that a captain should have the respect of

his peers. He need not be the best player on the field, but he must always be capable of setting an example and of leading by that example. A captain will not gain the respect of the rest of his team unless he is worth his place in the side. No team can afford to carry a man just because he is a good captain. You can carry a specialist player with limited ability in other spheres. You can, for instance, carry a very fast wing who lacks defensive ability, or a bean pole of a man who is expert at the line-out but is not a great all-round forward, or a fairly ordinary full-back who can kick goals from almost anywhere. You can do this because you can make more or less sure that other members of the team can cover up his deficiencies. But you cannot cover up for a captain. The captain must be looked up to by everyone.

A captain must also be something of a psychologist. He must

Surely the perfect instance of leading by example. Billy Beaumont crashes into Jim Renwick, supported by two of his most loyal henchmen, Roger Uttley and Fran Cotton

understand that some people need more stick than others —
some will respond to a quick word of encouragement, others
need to be sworn at. There is never much point, for instance, in
verbally assaulting a player who has dropped a pass. It is a safe
bet that he has not dropped the pass on purpose. If he is worth
his salt, he will be full of chagrin at having let the ball slip from
his grasp, and if you curse him you will only make his misery
worse so that he may well drop the next two passes as well.
What you should do is try to see why he has dropped the pass
and give him a friendly word of advice. If he respects you — as
he should do if you are a good captain — he will welcome your
advice and be thankful you have not given him a dressing-down.

So look for the reasons why the pass was dropped. Was it
because the player was watching his opposite number and
taking his eyes off the ball? Did he simply not have his hands
ready in a position to catch the pass? Was he thinking of some
complicated manoeuvre before he had become accustomed to
the tempo of the game? The captain must think of this kind of
thing and act accordingly.

*Willie John McBride
talks to his 1974
Lions at half-time*

Motivation. Fergus Slattery instills into his Ireland team what he wants them to do in the second half

There have been many captains — far too many — who have gone about the field haranguing and shouting at everybody indiscriminately and subsequently wondered why their team has not won more matches. A captain must have drive and the ability to communicate urgency, but he must also have tact and understanding of human nature. The shouting can often be left to the pack-leader while the captain operates in more subtle ways.

That is not to say that the captain does not have to stir up the emotions of his side. He has got to be a motivator. He has got to be able to pull together the fourteen other people in his team. Captaincy, in short, is no easy job, and it is especially important that the captain should maintain his own form. It is often said that the responsibility of captaining a side can spoil a man's play. This is certainly true of some players, but then they are not really good captains unless they can maintain their form while acting in the demanding role of captain.

Sometimes players are appointed captains simply because

they are acknowledged to be the best players in their teams. This certainly ought to ensure initial respect from the rest of the side which is important, but the man with the most skill or technique is by no means necessarily the best captain. If you have not got a true ability to lead you will very soon be found out, and all respect will vanish. There are few things more demoralising for a team than to realise that the man they have been looking up to is not in fact a good leader. Up to a point you can *become* a reasonably good leader simply through experience and knowledge of the game. But the time will come when it is vital to inspire, and the ability to inspire is given to relatively few people.

In that sense a captain must have a natural, rather than a manufactured, ease of command. A man who has not got that natural ability will get nowhere when the crunch comes. You cannot pretend to be a captain; there must be no play-acting. Indeed a captain must at all times be himself. It is perhaps the ability to expose and project his true self that most distinguishes a captain from the rest of his team-mates.

2 The Coach

At every level it is vital to success that the captain should be able to get on well with the coach. It is obvious that the two must co-operate closely and for a prolonged period of time at club level, but equally at international level it is no use appointing a captain who will not hit it off with the appointed coach. The two must have a happy relationship. At representative level it is all too easy to pick a captain who does not respect the appointed coach or does not even know him well. The captain and coach are together responsible for generating a good team atmosphere and developing co-operation among the individuals so as to produce a cohesive team effort.

At school level a coach, in relation to the captain and the team as a whole, tends to be autocratic, and a club coach may adopt a similar kind of attitude depending on the number of experienced players he has in his side and how experienced a player he is himself. In return a captain will have more respect for a coach who has played rugby at a high level than for one who is merely the holder of the Rugby Football Union Award Scheme badge. There are, of course, exceptions to this, among them Jack Rowell who coached Gosforth and then went south to Bath. He is a man who is widely liked and who can therefore get people to do what needs to be done. Respect from captain and players for a man like Rowell comes from his personality rather than from his record.

Gosforth found Rowell a very shrewd man-manager who could ease his way through most situations in the administration of the club. He used the expertise of the players available in the sense that they told him what was needed and he then produced plans based on the players' ideas. He would say, for instance, 'We're playing Coventry on Saturday. They're strong here and here and here, so what are you going to do about it?' In this way he got the players to think about their rugby.

Gosforth's next coach was Mick Mahoney who was a much more fiery head-on confrontation man. He was more authoritarian but he, too, got respect and results. Roger was captain under both Rowell and Mahoney and got on well with both of them: 'Mutual respect played a big part in all of this. I think they respected my ability to play rugby, and I respected Jack's superb wit and sense of humour, his ability to deal with people. I respected Mick for his hundred per cent honest approach and commitment to the team.' The point is that different people have different ways of motivating their teams, and what matters is that the captain and coach have a respectful and understanding relationship.

Some coaches can be more like a father figure. Roger recalls that when he first played county rugby for Northumberland, John Elders was something of a father figure: 'I leaned heavily on him, and it was good to be able to talk to someone like him.'

'The adviser to the captain' was the way the Scottish Rugby Union for a long time referred to Scotland's national coach, and they were held in derision by some people for doing so. 'Why can't they call a coach a coach?' people said. Yet in reality 'adviser to the captain' is not a bad definition of what a coach should be. Bad coaches overstep the mark and try to become dominant, but the captain must retain authority and responsibility for what happens on the field. Once the game has started, the captain is in charge. In the period of preparation before a match, in case of disagreement, the final say should still rest with the captain, not the coach.

Ideally, of course, there should be no disagreement between captain and coach, and the captain should help the coach by

Mike Davis, the England coach, directs a national squad session in 1980. Maurice Colclough, Billy Beaumont and John Scott attend

pointing out where the coach may, for instance, be training players too hard too short a time before the next match. John Dawes, when coach to the Lions in New Zealand in 1977, was always careful not to drive his players too hard on the Thursday before a Test Saturday. 'You can so easily leave it all on the paddock,' he used to say. But there was a certain New Zealand coach, who had better be nameless, who seemed to believe that fitness was everything. Even on the day before a big match he would insist on some hard training. The players hated it, knowing they were overdoing it; they lost their appetite and energy for the game, and this particular coach achieved poor results. He is probably still wondering why. Now, in such a situation it is surely the duty of the captain to help his coach by speaking out on behalf of the players and telling him he is overdoing it. A coach who is any good at all will listen to what the captain has to say and will take the advice offered.

As in most walks of life, a sense of humour is an essential quality for a coach to possess. Fred Allen, the astonishingly successful coach to Auckland and the All Blacks, had a reputation for driving his men very hard on the training ground and for singling out players for extra runs and sprints. But when Allen was coach to the All Blacks, Brian Lochore, the New Zealand captain, was a big enough man to get through to Allen's sense of humour and, as a result of Lochore's prompting, the players felt no lasting resentment at what to some players from Britain would have appeared to be bullying methods by Allen.

It is tempting to conclude that players from different countries respond to different types of coaching — that the English, for example, will get on better with a quieter, more reasoning and less flamboyant style of coaching. Yet there have been 'loud' coaches who have got results with English sides, and there have also been quietly spoken and relatively gentle New

18

Zealanders who have produced successful All Black teams. After the noisy coaching of Fred Allen and Ivan Vodanovich it was a surprise to find the mild manner of J.J. Stewart when he coached the All Blacks on their visit to celebrate Ireland's centenary. He and the captain, Andy Leslie, worked closely together on the training field, and you felt that J.J. really was an adviser to the captain. Jack Gleeson, coach to the All Blacks in France in 1977 and in the British Isles in 1978, was another relatively quiet man who seemed to be able to get the best out of New Zealanders without adopting a sergeant-major attitude. Again, one of the reasons for the successes of his teams was his close relationship with his captain, Graham Mourie.

3 Tactics

One of the charms of rugby is the infinite variety of strategy and tactics it affords, and it is one of the main duties of the captain, working in conjunction with his coach and discussing matters with his own players, to make decisions about which tactics to use. The coach can help with these decisions before the game starts, but once play has begun, the responsibility for changing or adapting plans is the captain's alone. Basically, what a captain aims to do is to discover and exploit weaknesses in the opposing team, at the same time blunting the effectiveness of his opponents' relative points of strength. He will also be seeking to do the converse: to make the utmost use of his own team's strengths while hiding his side's weak points. If, for instance, your opponents have a pack of forwards who are very strong scrummagers, you may decide to put the ball into the scrums immediately the two front rows have come together so as to deny your opponents the chance to push your forwards back.

The tossing of the coin by the two captains before the kick-off is more important in rugby than in some other sports because the weather conditions can have such a profound effect on play. Remember that the captain, on winning the toss, has the right to decide either which end of the field to play from or to do the kicking-off. On a windless day with no sun the captain may choose to kick off, but very often there is wind or sun to be taken into consideration.

If there is a strong wind blowing down the pitch, the captain

may prefer to have the wind behind his team in the first half. A rugby ball is big enough and light enough to be greatly influenced by the wind when in the air, and it is common practice for a captain, on winning the toss, to allow his team the advantage of having the wind behind them when all his players are fresh. He may thus hope that his team will score a large number of points in the first half, giving his men a psychological advantage with which to face the wind in the second half.

Some captains argue that it is more sensible to play against the wind in the first half when their players are at their freshest and have lots of energy to devote to defence. They believe that in the second half their team will then have the wind behind them as an aid when they are feeling more tired. This school of thought also maintains that, since relatively few opportunities for scoring arise in the first twenty minutes or so of a match, it

21

is a waste of resources to have the use of the wind in this period. Such a policy, however, depends upon the ability of the side playing against the wind in the first half to prevent their opponents from building up the psychological advantage of a big score.

On a grey November afternoon in Britain it is difficult to imagine that the sun can have much influence on a game of rugby. But there are sunny days in Britain, and in many overseas countries the position of the sun has to be taken into account in almost every game. The sun can be an important factor, for instance, when the ball is kicked high and a defender has the sun in his eyes when he tries to catch it.

If there is a bright sun shining from end to end of the pitch, a captain will normally decide to play with it behind his team in the first half. In this way he is sure of being able to take advantage of the sun which may go behind clouds later in the game. Occasionally exceptional circumstances may be met in which the sun, while not in a position to influence play at the beginning of a game, may do so later as it moves across the sky. In such circumstances a captain will make sure that his own team do not have to play towards the low sun in the second half.

According to the orientation of the pitch, you can also get a situation in which a low sun is shining across the pitch, rather than from end to end, in the later stages of a game. The 1968 Lions in South Africa missed what appeared from the stand to be a simple try in a Test because of a low sun shining across the pitch. Bob Taylor, the England flanker, was unmarked at the back of a line-out near the Springbok goal-line, and the ball was thrown in straight to him. But the ball came to him right out of the evening sun and he could not judge its flight.

When the players have the wind behind them, it is important that they should make full use of this advantage. The most obvious way of doing so is by long punting from the half-backs so as to gain positions deep in the opposing half of the field where a ruck, maul or line-out may take place within easy striking distance of the opponents' goal-line. Punting with the wind can also lead to almost constant occupation of enemy territory, thus increasing the likelihood of feasible penalty kicks and dropped goals. In addition, a high punt towards the opposing posts may well cause difficulties for the defending full-back as he tries in vain to judge the flight of the ball. Under pressure from those who are following up the kick, the full-back may drop the ball, thus presenting loose possession to his opponents. A kicker with the sun behind him should similarly make use of high punts which a defender will find awkward to field as the ball arrives from out of the sun. The wind, of course, can also be of use in defence because if the ball is kicked high into the air from a defensive position, it will travel with the wind a long way downfield, banishing the attackers' threat.

Rain and a wet field also have to be taken into account when strategy is being decided. When the ball is wet and slippery it is difficult for the threequarters to pass it with accuracy, so that in such conditions it is often advisable to try to make progress through the punting of the half-backs rather than through passing. Since it is also difficult to gather a slippery ball when it is rolling on a wet pitch, it is a sensible attacking strategy to kick the ball along the ground for the attacking side to chase.

The important thing to remember about methods of playing rugby is that they are constantly evolving. A particular style of tactics is effective for a period, but then defences become alerted and there is the need to develop new methods. In the distant past, play seems to have been largely confined to the forwards, with backs very occasionally being brought into the game. Then for a long period, roughly during the first half of the twentieth century, the duty of the forwards was, generally, to provide possession for the backs to use. More recently there has been a swing back to the idea of forwards having most of the play and backs running only when the field in front of them has been broken.

It is also important to remember that there is nothing inherently wrong with tactics based on punting by the half-backs. In fact certain weather conditions demand such methods as sometimes do the relative strengths and weaknesses of the two teams who are taking part in a match. If you have strong forwards and unskilled backs and your opponents have incisive backs but weak forwards, then your captain should decide to keep play tight so that your forward strength can be brought to bear on the issue of the game and your relative weakness at threequarter remain unexploited by the opposition.

24

There was a classic example of a team using the wrong tactics when Scotland played the All Blacks at Murrayfield in 1979. One of the strengths of those All Blacks was their general mobility and the swiftness with which they could make the most of mistakes by opposing backs. In the first quarter of the game the Scotland forwards were well on top at the set pieces, and Scotland's tactics should have been to play to this advantage they had gained forward. But instead of keeping play largely confined to their forwards by getting their half-backs to bring play back to their pack, Scotland tried to play an expansive, open game to which their backs were unsuited. The Scottish half-backs either passed the ball to centres who dropped it, or else they punted the ball ahead to an All Black defence deployed to profit by running in counter-attack. Thus, whether the Scottish half-backs passed the ball to their unreliable centres or kicked it ahead, it was the All Blacks who always benefited from the possession hard won by the Scottish forwards. Not surprisingly the Scottish forwards gradually wilted as they saw all this possession squandered and once Graham Mourie, the All Blacks captain, switched to mini line-outs and so brought to an end the Scottish domination of this branch of play, there was no way Scotland could win. Had Scotland played tight rugby from the start, they might well have gained an early lead and held out for victory. The moral of that game was that there is no point in playing open rugby for open rugby's sake. A captain's tactics should be based on the relative strengths and weaknesses of the two teams when they are playing on the day.

It is all too easy for any particular method of play to become something of an obsession. The 1963-64 All Blacks in Britain made a great thing of creating second-phase possession. A favourite method was to get their second five-eighth, or inside centre, to run either inwards or straight ahead into a tackle so that the forwards could rush in and win the ball from the subsequent ruck. These methods were seen at their most effective when the Lions went to New Zealand in 1966 and lost all four Tests against the All Blacks. By then the New Zealanders were setting up ruck after ruck and only releasing the ball to their backs when they had pinned one or two of the opposing backs to the ground in a ruck. Thus the All Black backs would outnumber their opponents and have little difficulty in running over for tries.

British rugby intelligently analysed these All Black methods and imitated them. The British teams who really concentrated on this style of play were rewarded with success. But, as happens so often, the imitation was overdone to the extent that variations to these methods were overlooked and forgotten.

The irony was that when the All Blacks returned to Britain in 1967 they themselves played a much more expansive type of rugby, frequently setting their threequarters into action directly from set pieces. The point is that they knew they had skilful backs on that tour and were determined to make the utmost use of them. The result was that they went through their tour unbeaten.

British rugby's obsession with getting centres to set up second-phase possession by running inwards so as to be within reach of the breaking forwards has led to a neglect of the previously accepted fundamentals of threequarter play by which midfield backs went for the outside gaps and tried to fashion overlaps for their open-side wing threequarters. This has meant that British midfield defences, having become inured to a system in which opponents run straight at them, have been dumbfounded by opponents from overseas who have tried the old method of running at the gap rather than at the man.

It is not easy for the captain and coach of a club to do more than make the best use of the fairly limited talent at their disposal. But tactics should remain as flexible as possible so that the element of surprise is readily available, and, of course, any novelty should be encouraged and put into practice. Gloucester, for some years, had a plan at line-outs in which the

26

The pack-leader has his say. Terry Cobner, whose tuition and example meant so much to the 1977 Lions pack in New Zealand, talks to his men at half-time

ball was given to John Watkins, the flanker, who had positioned himself so as to peel round the front of the line-out, close to the touchline. Although the move became known to Gloucester's opponents it remained effective, especially when preceded by a brief dummy peel round the back by someone else.

And then there is the example of Tarbes, the French club, who had a powerful pack of forwards and a capable scrum-half but no other adequate backs apart from an international right-wing threequarter. Tarbes devised and rehearsed a move in which when the scrum-half got the ball from his pack, he immediately kicked it low and straight across the field between the opposing threequarter lines. The ideal was that it would bounce and roll towards the far touchline where it would be gathered by their international wing threequarter in full stride. What is more the move worked and frequently produced tries. It was a good example of surprise and at the same time of making the best use of limited material.

Captains, in conjunction with coaches, should encourage their players to think up moves of this kind whose novelty will take opponents by surprise. Far too much rugby is predictable

27

and therefore easily defended against. A little bit of originality, or even a switch back to a previous style of play, can make all the difference between victory and defeat.

As an example of switching back to former methods you could not do better than study the play of the Australian Schools team who toured the British Isles in the 1977-78 season. They began their tour by beating London Counties Schools 54-6, they beat the Midlands 63-12 and they beat England 31-9. They won all their fourteen games, scoring 479 points with only 93 against. Moreover, they scored 103 tries in those fourteen games and conceded only five.

The main feature of the Australians' play was the quickness of their passing. Nowhere was this more marked than at scrum-half where length was shamelessly sacrificed in favour of quickness. In British rugby in general there has been great emphasis placed in recent years on the need for length in a scrum-half's pass. But, logically, if a full threequarter movement is carried out, this extra length in the scrum-half's pass puts the open-side wing threequarter that much nearer the touchline, giving him less room for manoeuvre.

These Australians used short passes all along the line with the result that their wing threequarter received the ball with all the space in the world in which to beat his man or to be supported on the outside by his full-back. This was the kind of space that used to be given to open-side wing threequarters in the days when forwards were considered to be the people who did little more than provide clean possession for their backs to use with running and passing. In other words, the play of these highly successful Australian schoolboys was a throwback to another age. And because it was a type of rugby with which the current generation was unfamiliar, there was no immediate counter to it. So, while novelty is important, it should be remembered by captains and coaches, at all levels of the game, that a revival of some of the methods of the past can prove equally effective.

Captains should also remember the dropped goal as an

important psychological weapon. Your side may be pressing and attacking for a long period but, being met by a stubborn defence, may not be able to score any points. This can become frustrating for your team, especially for the forwards who have been winning lots of possession, and it can be encouraging for the morale of your opponents because they feel that their defence is impregnable and that in time your efforts will die out and their turn will come to attack. Then suddenly one of your half-backs drops a goal, and you have got three points which your opponents' defence was powerless to prevent. This can have a profound psychological effect on your opponents because they realise all the effort and energy they have been expending in defence has failed to prevent you from taking a lead.

Pierre Albaladejo, the French fly-half, who once dropped three goals in a match against Ireland, was a great believer in the psychological value of the drop-kick. He, incidentally, was also a very reliable place-kicker who was never put off by the noisy French crowds who used to screech when he was taking kicks at goal in club matches. In fact he said that when he toured with the French team in New Zealand what put him off more than anything else was the deathly silence in which the well-mannered New Zealand crowds used to allow him to take his goal-kicks.

Sometimes a captain will have to play in a match without knowing much about the strengths and weaknesses of his opponents beforehand. At other times he will know quite a lot about his opponents, and he and the coach will have been able to plan their strategy and tactics accordingly. If you know nothing or very little about your opponents, you should concentrate on making use of your own team's points of strength to start with, at the same time probing for weaknesses in your opponents. If, for instance, you have a very good right-wing threequarter, try all the methods you can think of to bring him into the play. You will have thought of these beforehand, and all your team should know about them, because they will form part of your regular tactics. If you have reliable handlers in your centre, you can try getting the ball to your wing by means of orthodox passing along the threequarter line. The centres should have been reminded before the game that, in such movements, they should not just pass the ball slavishly along the line: if a gap appears in front of one of them, he must take it. And, of course, the movement can be varied by bringing the full-back into the line so as to give your wing an overlap or at least an edge.

Try bringing your wing into the game at times when he is operating on the blind side. If you have room you can, for instance, get your fly-half or full-back to take the scrum-half's pass on the blind side and feed the wing in that way. Alternatively your scrum-half can run on the blind side and

your wing can support him, or one of your flankers can move out from the pack and take his scrum-half's pass, then linking with the wing threequarter.

Your No.8, too, can be encouraged to pick up the ball from a scrum and make off on the blind side with the idea of linking with the wing. This is a particularly good idea if the blind side is narrow. If there is more room, your scrum-half and loose forwards can try out a varied programme of combined moves on the blind side so as to bring your wing threequarter into the game. Your wing himself can be told to leave the blind side position and rush into the back line, probably next to the fly-half. If he does this surreptitiously, he may be able to run clean through the first line of defence. It is usually worth having a go in a situation like this because the worst that is likely to happen is that the wing will create a ruck or maul favourable to your pack.

You can also try to bring your wing threequarter into the game by means of various punts executed by your fly-half. The most obvious kicks are the long, diagonal kick when your wing is on the open side of the field and then, when he is on the blind side, the tactic in which your fly-half runs to the open side and punts the ball up the blind side for your wing to run on to.

While you, as captain, are trying out methods of bringing your own team's strengths into the proceedings, weaknesses will probably be appearing in your opponents' side. The weaknesses may be individual (e.g. a weak tackler) or they may be collective (perhaps slow-witted defence around scrums). The important thing is that you as captain must be watching all the time for any such weaknesses to appear, and you must remember them for exploitation later in the game.

If no obvious weaknesses have appeared you could try, for instance, putting the opposing full-back through a searching test. Your fly-half or scrum-half might try bombarding him with high punts so placed that either your forwards or your centres can arrive in the vicinity of the catcher at the same time as the ball. The nerve of many a full-back has been known to crack when he has become aware of a Tony Bond rushing in to tackle him. Gloucester, too, used to test the courage of opposing full-backs by sending up high punts and getting that rugged centre, John Bayliss, to harrass the opposing full-back.

If the full-back proves to be shaky, go on testing him and you will probably get some loose possession with which to score a try or else a scrum near his line from which to go for a try or penalty kick at goal because a hard pressed supporting defender has illegally killed the ball in the loose. If, on the other hand, the opposing full-back is found to be courageous and faultless in his catching and gathering, try putting your punts between the full-back and his wing threequarter to see if their combined defensive drill is sound. If there is any misunderstanding you could, again, be presented with loose possession with which to go for a try.

The important thing is to go on pressing and probing. You can, for instance, test your opponents' direct midfield defence by telling your own midfield players to chance their arm. Your centres can go for the outside gap and then for the inside gap while you, the captain, watch for any signs of weakness. If you have a powerful centre of the Tony Bond type, you could get him to run hard and straight and see if there is any evidence of flinching on the part of the defender. In the same way your centres and fly-half can attempt various 'scissors' moves and perhaps a loop by the fly-half (where he passes the ball on and then runs swiftly round the back and comes into the line again for a pass).

Do not forget the possibility of bringing your full-back into the line at various places and at various angles. If you have ever watched J.P.R. Williams or Andy Irvine you will know what that means. Instead of bringing the full-back in as an extra centre so as to give your open-side wing threequarter an overlap, you can, for example, get him to run inwards for a scissors move or a short pass on the burst from one of the centres or from your fly-half. In this way you can find out if your opponents are organised to deal with such moves. If they are not, then try again in a different place and at a different angle. Keep them guessing.

Another important area in which you should test your opponents' defensive organisation is on the fringes of the pack. You can get your scrum-half to try to break and make sure that his attempt is closely supported by your loose forwards. Or you can get your scrum-half and a flanker to launch a combined thrust close to the pack. Get your No.8 and scrum-half to attack together in a similar move. Or tell, say, your right-hand flanker at a set scrum to run quickly round behind the scrum to the left and take a pass from his scrum-half on the way.

From line-outs try out any of the peeling moves you will have rehearsed under the guidance of your coach. If you are getting nowhere with peeling moves round the back of the line-out, remember that a sudden peel round the front, perhaps preceded by a feint to peel round the back, may catch the opposing defence unawares. The French, with Lucian Mias, their big lock forward, as the spearhead made a great success of peeling round the back in the late 1950s.

Phil Bennett tells the 1977 Lions what he wants from them in the second half against Bay of Plenty

Your forwards will, by direct confrontation, be discovering the strengths and weaknesses of the opposing pack in the more static phases of play. If your forwards are stronger than their opponents at the scrums, for instance, you should try to exploit this advantage by driving them off the ball, or by checking your shove in mid-stream and shoving again even harder, or by turning their scrum when they put the ball in. Remember how the Irish and French packs were manipulated and out-manoeuvred by the 1980 England forwards in this way so that such talented running scrum-halves as Colin Patterson of Ireland and Jerome Gallion of France were kept almost completely in check. Make your opponents keep down in scrummages for as long as you can so that you can tire them out with your superior strength and techniques.

On your own put-in you can exploit your advantage at the scrums by, for instance, driving ahead and getting your No.8 to pick up the ball and charge forward with it. Near your opponents' line you can often get a try in this way because the opposing loose forwards will be forced to help hold your shove, and the weight and momentum of your No.8 may well carry him over the goal-line, even if not all the immediate defence is committed to scrummaging. And if your opponents attempt to check the effect of your pack's shove by collapsing the scrum (illegal and dangerous) you should at least get a penalty goal, if not a penalty try. Remember, too, the possibility of scoring a pushover try. If you really have a marked advantage at the scrums, you may be able to detach a flanker and get your scrum-half to pass the ball direct to him. England have used Tony Neary in this way.

If, however, you find your opponents are stronger than you are at the scrums, you should tell your pack to stay in the scrums for as short a time as possible. One way of ensuring this, on your own put-in, is to tell your scrum-half to put the ball in the instant the two front rows come together for the forming of the scrum. In this way you seek to deny your opponents the chance to make their weight and strength tell against your weaker pack. The New Zealand Universities, who beat the 1977 Lions 21-6 at Christchurch, did this most effectively, and Japanese teams, with their small stature, have used these methods to offset their obvious physical disadvantage.

If you find you have an advantage in height at the line-out, exploit this advantage with drives and peels. Perhaps it is clear from the start that your men at the back of the line-out are taller than theirs. If so, make full use of the long throw-in to the back of the line remembering, however, that it is not easy to throw the ball to the back of the line straight if there is a strong wind.

On the other hand, if your opponents are taller than your men at the line-out and appear to be well drilled, tell your half-backs not to kick to touch. If they do kick to touch, this means there will be a lot of line-outs, and your opponents will be able to exploit their advantage. And if your opponents have a clear advantage in height at the back of the line-out and are using this for gaining possession or for launching peels, send one of your locks back to police the back of the line.

If you find your opponents' forwards are slow-moving, try playing an expansive, open game so that you can outpace them, at the same time forcing their cumbersome forwards to run about the field and so become tired and therefore less effective at the set pieces. If, on the other hand, their forwards turn out to be quicker than yours, keep play tight. You can do this by playing ten-man or even nine-man rugby so that your slower forwards are not caught at a disadvantage in the open.

The higher the level at which you are playing, the more you probably know about your opponents beforehand and the more they probably know about your team. This applies especially, of course, if you are playing in international rugby because you can watch television or video versions of games in which your opponents have already taken part. When you know how your opponents are likely to want to play the game, you can make detailed plans in advance. If, for instance, you are going to play against a team whose coach and captain probably know that you have a full-back who is an uncertain fielder of the ball, then you must emphasise to your wing threequarters the importance of covering and supporting your full-back.

However thoroughly you may make plans in advance, be prepared to change your methods and tactics in mid-stream. There was a good example of such a change when Scotland played the 1979 All Blacks at Murrayfield. The New Zealand captain, Graham Mourie, probably thought that with Andy Haden in the middle of his line-up the All Blacks would be able to beat Scotland at the line-out. But in the first half Scotland won considerably more good possession from the line-outs than the All Blacks. So Mourie changed his methods and called for mini line-outs. As a result of this decision the Scots were deprived of their earlier advantage at the line-outs, and this was one reason why the All Blacks got well on top in the second half.

The more familiar the two opposing teams are with each other's methods of play the more important it is for you, as captain, to produce the unexpected. You probably will not be able to make a complete change of style, but do try an occasional sudden thrust which is totally out of character with what your opponents will know to be your customary style.

There was a classic example of this when the All Blacks played the 1977 Lions in the third Test at Carisbrook, Dunedin. The All Blacks were generally expected to play a fairly tight, spoiling type of game, and such expectations were only increased by the sight of the soft mud of the Carisbrook pitch. Many people thought the All Blacks would rue their selectors' decision to drop Sid Going for this Test, for Lyn Davis, his successor at scrum-half, was not known for his ability to dictate the tight kind of play demanded by the awkward conditions. Yet from the very start the All Blacks defied the conditions with open, attacking rugby which so startled the Lions that the

All Blacks scored a try within forty-five seconds of the kick-off. What is more the All Blacks' running rugby, exposing flaws in the defence of the Lions' backs, brought them victory by 19-7 and a 2-1 lead in the four-match Test series.

Another good example of an unexpected switch in tactics, again concerning a change at scrum-half, was when the French went to Cardiff Arms Park to play Wales in 1960. That year France had already beaten Scotland 13-11 at Murrayfield and drawn 3-3 with England in Paris, and they had an excellent and thoroughly experienced scrum-half in Pierre Danos who had won seventeen caps. Everyone was shocked when Danos was dropped for the French match in Cardiff because nobody would believe that the French selectors could have found another scrum-half to match the quality of Danos.

But when the game got under way it became clear why the French selectors had called in Pierre Lacroix at scrum-half. They had reasoned that the home countries by now knew that France, with a fluent passer like Danos at scrum-half, would concentrate on giving the ball quickly to their talented three-quarters. They reasoned, too, that the Welsh would counter by mounting an aggressive spoiling defence against the French threequarters, aiming to force them into uncertain handling. What was apparent within a few minutes of the kick-off at Cardiff was that the new French scrum-half was not interested in threequarter play. He was a sturdy, chunky little man whose first thought always was to run, or at least to probe for openings in the company of his loose forwards.

His three loose forwards were very good players indeed. Michel Crauste eventually won 43 caps, Michel Celaya 35, and François Moncla 21. In this match at Cardiff they combined superbly with their scrum-half and France scored four tries, one by Lacroix himself, one by Celaya and one by each of the wing threequarters on the blind side. Instead of the anticipated threequarter movements the French used their new scrum-half and their loose forwards for practically all their attacking moves. Wales were beaten 16-8 and France went on to defeat the Welsh four years on the trot. So a captain should never forget the importance of surprise and the unexpected.

If you find yourself playing against a side who are better than you at the set scrums and line-outs with the result that you are more or less starved of possession, you will clearly have to devise a means of forcing your opponents to make mistakes in the loose so as to present your team with loose possession. Remember also not to waste the ball when you get it at kick-offs, drop-outs, tapped penalties and free kicks, and from your opponents' missed kicks at goal. If you are short of set-piece possession, it is vital to make use of every scrap of possession you can get from other sources.

Gerald Davies was one player who hated to waste an opportunity of this sort. On one occasion, playing for the English Universities against the Welsh Universities at Birkenhead — this was in his Loughborough days — he caught the ball behind his own line from an opponent's kick at goal which missed. Running out from behind the line, he darted past those opponents who had followed up the kick, accelerated past others and threaded his way through the remaining defenders for a try behind the posts. That was an exciting example of exceptional individual talent put to best use. Admittedly not many teams can boast of a side-stepper of anything approaching that quality. But, with imaginative and disciplined support play, it is perfectly possible to attack in a broken field from near your own line. Remember that famous try, started by Phil Bennett and finished by Gareth Edwards, in the Barbarians' match against the All Blacks at Cardiff in 1973.

Few teams make full use of their ability at the line-out, so the captain should help the coach to think up variations, including getting the players to switch positions. Here we can learn a lot from the Japanese whose small physique has of necessity made them inventive. They cannot hope to compete physically, so they have had to use their brains. One of their

early methods was to get their man at the front of the line-out to duck while a fast, low, torpedo throw-in whistled over him to a team-mate who would stretch forward and deflect the ball to the scrum-half. On England's tour in 1979 the Japanese went so far as to get their man at the front to leap into the air so that the ball could be thrown in low and underneath him to the next man who would dive to the ground and sweep the ball to the scrum-half. They even had a move in which a fast, low throw-in was nudged to the scrum-half not by the hands but deliberately by the leg of the line-out player. This calls for a quick eye and considerable agility on the part of the scrum-half!

If you are managing to use your threequarters for full movements out to the open-side wing threequarter, and you notice that your opponents are all streaming across the field to provide a quick cover defence, remind your wing of the possibility of trying a cross-kick. A cross-kick from the wing towards the posts has the effect of forcing the coverers to alter course and go back towards the middle of the field. In the meantime some of your men, anticipating the cross-kick, are already going towards the opposition's posts. They will thus have a start over the covering opponents and will arrive at the spot where the ball lands in an attacking situation, the opponents being in the position of having to scramble back towards their own line.

The incredibly successful Lourdes team, who won the French club championship six times in nine years, used to score a lot of tries as a result of cross-kicks. Their threequarters were made to line back really steeply to make sure that their centres had plenty of room in which to take and give their passes without worrying about the possibility of being tackled in possession. The open-side wing threequarter saw a lot of the ball — and his opponents expected him to do so. The opposing cover, therefore, was often quickly across the field, at least early in the game before the Lourdes type of running rugby had had its effect of tiring opponents in the chase. So the open-side wing would cross kick and the great Jean Prat, or one of the other Lourdes forwards, would score near the posts. The French national team likewise made use of a large number of cross-kicks the day they beat England 13-0 in Paris in 1962. That was the occasion when Michel Crauste, the flanker, scored three tries.

If you find that your opponents' centres are coming up very quickly in defence and are harrassing your centres, the routine thing for you to do is to tell your fly-half to kick the ball over the heads of the opposing advancing centres. This may mean that one of your centres can reach the ball while it is in the gap behind the opposing centres and in front of the full-back, and it may persuade the opposition centres not to come up quite so quickly in future. But remember to look also for a gap through which your fly-half might be able to run. If opposing centres come up really quickly in defence, it is quite possible they have done so more quickly than their fly-half, thus spoiling the alignment of their backs as a whole. In such a case your fly-half might well be able to slip through the gap outside his opposite number and behind the inside-centre.

Do remember that fast, aggressive defence by the opposing centres can also be defeated by the method used by Lourdes i.e. getting your own centres to line back really steeply. People often speak strongly against steep alignment, saying that if one of your centres drops the ball in such a formation your forwards will be at a great disadvantage because they will have to be covering back towards their own line in their attempt to recover the loose ball. This is true, but why should you assume that one of your centres will drop the ball? If your coach has made your backs do a lot of practising of taking and giving passes and if your centres line back so steeply that they have plenty of space in which to accomplish their handling under no pressure, surely it is pessimistic to assume that one or other of them will let the ball slip from his grasp.

4 Captaincy at School

The captaincy of a school side can be of immense benefit to the new captain. The job may give him his first opportunity of acquiring a true sense of responsibility, and it will make him realise and appreciate the interdependent community which is a good school. He will have to work closely with the master who is doing the coaching, and this will help him to become aware of the self-sacrifice that teachers make in the interests of their charges. The captaincy of a school team can therefore be an important agent in broadening a boy's mind.

But the school rugby captain will be aware, or should be, that he himself has to give a lot of his time and his energies to the job. By and large, the more he puts into it the more he will get out of it. If he is lucky his coach will want to discuss not only the playing ability of his team-mates but also their characters and their reaction under stress and the pressures of a close game. This can lead to a close relationship with the coach, affording the boy an insight into the real meaning of education.

It can be seen from this that the role of school coach is a vital one, for the coach can have a profound effect on the captain. The two must work closely together if their team is to be successful, and the coach must be sure that the captain is allowed the freedom to switch tactics in the middle of the battle.

Probably at school level more than at any other level the outstanding athlete is made captain. This may work because the athlete may also be a natural leader, but often it does not. The

outstanding athlete may be too concerned about his own performance to be able to devote enough time to the general well-being of his side.

Similarly, there is always the temptation in school rugby to appoint the senior player left over from the previous season as captain. This has the initial advantage that your experienced player will be looked up to by the rest of the team, but it could be a disastrous choice in the long run when experience is found to be no substitute for the natural ability to lead, so it should not be done as a matter of course.

There is a problem here because if you do not appoint as captain the senior boy remaining from the previous season, you may do considerable damage to that boy's self-respect. In certain cases it may even be better to put up with a less than

They start rugby young in New Zealand. John Dawes, coach to the 1977 Lions, has an attentive crowd of spectators for a training session at Christchurch

inspiring captain rather than to risk damaging the self-confidence of a young man. Ideally the born leaders in the school should be spotted young, long before they reach the school's first team, so that they can be guided into such positions where they become the clearly accepted leading candidates for the captaincy. They should also be given opportunities to captain sides lower down the school so that they can learn the techniques of leadership through which to direct their natural ability towards the best interests of their team.

If the school team is taken to see a big match — say, an international or a game involving a team like the Barbarians or the Irish Wolfhounds — it is a good idea for the captain to sit or stand next to his school coach so that they can discuss the various strengths and weaknesses of the two teams and also the intelligent moves and the faults. Watching a match in this critical way is one of the best means of acquiring a knowledge of rugby and so of obtaining the judgment needed by a true captain. Superficially it may not seem such fun as just cheering and yelling your head off, but in the long term it can be very much more rewarding.

There are a multitude of jobs which the school rugby captain has to carry out. He may well find himself responsible for collecting the strips and for such important functions as organising fixtures. He is also bound to be asked to help in the selection of the school team. The degree to which his advice is sought will depend on the attitude of the coach, but a good coach will want to work closely in harmony with the captain. Remember, too, to make sure the players know they have been selected.

Roger can well remember his own school days and says he was not really interested in rugby when he went to secondary school:

'A lot of friends were involved in soccer and naturally I wanted to play with them. Unfortunately in our first game against local opposition the four-foot midgets in their attack tore the eleven-year-old, six-feet donkey to pieces, and I decided, along with the coaches, that perhaps rugby might be more my line of country.

'In those early days it used to be a little like Gulliver striding through the Lilliputians, and consequently I was given the captaincy on the grounds that I used to see quite a lot of the ball. In that first year I can remember being on the end of a hiding from the local grammar school. But by the time we had all reached the fifth form we were committed sportsmen, accomplished not only in the arts of rugby football but in basketball as well. So it was that we came to thrash the grammar school at basketball and then actually had the audacity to beat them at rugby. That is one of the outstanding memories of my schooldays.

'It was at this time that I came to realise that, as in playing so with captaincy, there is no substitute for experience. During all this period at school I was learning a lot and, having been

The perfect hand-off by Mike Slemen, the England wing who also coaches rugby at Merchant Taylors' Crosby

used to captaining teams at school for some time, it was a bit difficult when playing representative rugby for the first time not to feel almost affronted at not being appointed captain.'

A captain must be careful to give his side enthusiasm through encouragement rather than to reduce their performance by blaming them for errors. This sounds obvious, but it is all too easy to curse players for their mistakes and so to turn them off rather than on. For instance, it is not helpful for a captain who is a forward to make a collective condemnation of the backs if they have done something wrong. Even if a threequarter movement has lost twenty-five yards through poor alignment or erratic handling so that the forwards, who have worked hard for possession of the ball, have to trail back towards their own line, it is no help if the captain expresses the pack's frustration by swearing at the backs. They will be sore enough already at having let the forwards down. If he could see what went wrong, the captain should have a quick word with the leader of the backs, suggesting how to correct the fault.

The same applies in reverse. If the captain is a back and his forwards are under so much pressure that they have not managed to provide a regular supply of the ball from the set pieces, it is no use yelling at the pack collectively and demanding that they produce the ball more often. They will not be denying the backs the ball on purpose. You can take it that they are trying their hardest, and if you, a back who appears to be doing much less hard work than they are, start complaining at them, you can scarcely expect them to continue giving you wholehearted devotion. You will have lost their respect. Again, try to see how they might profitably channel their efforts along different lines, and have a word with the leader about it.

The captain should work out before the game starts how he is going to replace players in an emergency. If, as can happen to the best of us, a player has to go off for medical attention for ten minutes or so, how are you going to re-arrange your team during his absence? There are fairly obvious alterations you can make. If you lose a prop, for instance, you can move one of your locks into the front row and bring your No.8 to lock.

Similarly, if you loose your hooker you can get one of your props to hook and, again, bring a lock to prop and the No.8 to lock. If you lose your No.8, there may be some circumstances in which, instead of simply doing without a man in the No.8 position at scrums, you may need to ask one of your flankers to pack there. In the same way, if you lose a flanker you may, in certain circumstances, need your No.8 to pack down as a flanker.

Scrum-half is probably the most difficult position of all to fill in an emergency because it is such a specialist position. Usually a flanker is called upon to act as temporary scrum-half, but a shrewd captain will know in advance if any member of his team has ever operated as a scrum-half. The captain may have discovered that the fly-half or a centre or wing or even the full-back, has had some experience as a scrum-half. If so, this is the man to move to scrum-half in an emergency. It is not by any means an easy position to fill, and anyone who has had any experience of it at all, even just one or two games, should be your man to call on in an emergency.

The usual procedure for replacing a fly-half in an emergency is to call up one of the centres, bringing in a wing to fill the subsequent gap in the centre and putting a flanker out on the wing. But this is not the only way of dealing with the situation. You may have a wing threequarter who has played at fly-half in the past, and if you bring him to fly-half and put a flanker in his place on the wing you leave your centre pairing undisturbed. The Barbarians did this in their annual match against Leicester in 1979. Gareth Davies, the Welsh fly-half, had to go off with a leg injury, and the Barbarians brought Mike Slemen, the England wing, to fly-half.

Again, if you move a centre to fly-half you need not necessarily then move a wing into the centre and put a flanker on the wing. It depends on the capabilities of the players concerned. When Phil Horrocks-Taylor, the England fly-half, had to go off during England's match against the 1957-58 Wallabies at Twickenham, England's captain, Eric Evans, moved Jeff Butterfield from centre to fly-half but decided not to bring one of his wings into the centre to replace Butterfield. Instead he put one of his flankers, Peter Robbins, in the centre. This proved a shrewd move because Robbins was an excellent taker and giver of passes, and it was in this formation that England achieved a famous victory by 9-6 — Peter Jackson, the right-wing threequarter, settling the issue with a great try. Moreover this took place before it was permitted by the International Board to bring on substitutes.

The normal procedure for replacing a centre in an emergency is to bring in a wing threequarter and put a flanker on the wing. But, again, if you have a flanker who can handle soundly, it might be a better arrangement to put him in the centre and leave your wings undisturbed.

If you have to cope with the temporary loss of a wing three-quarter, you have not much option but to send a flanker to fill the position. However, the loss of a full-back can be dealt with in several ways. Probably the most normal way is to send a centre to full-back, bring a wing into the centre and put a flanker on the wing. But it is not unknown for the No.8 to be taken out of the pack and sent to full-back. Your decision will depend on the way the game is developing and on your knowledge of the capabilities of every member of your side. If, for example, you have been reaping reward from a policy of all-out attack, making full use of all your backs, you might find it worthwhile to move a wing threequarter to full-back (putting a flanker in his place on the wing) so that his pace can be used in the full-back's role of attacker and counter-attacker.

The important thing is that the captain should know his players well enough to be able to draw up his plans for emergencies before the start of the game. If you have any doubts, talk them over with the coach who will have been able to evaluate the capabilities of every player with more of the eye of an expert than you could yourself. It is also a good idea to let your vice-captain know your plans for dealing with emergencies. Not only that, your vice-captain should be kept thoroughly in the picture concerning your tactical plans and everything else. You never know when you yourself might have to go off the field.

5 Club Captaincy

In some ways being captain of a club is the most difficult type of captaincy. It is true that you have a lot of other club officials to help you with the off-the-field duties, but a club captain is expected to do so many varied jobs within the club that a great deal of energy and patience is required. The club captain has to sit on the various committees who run the club, and he will also be expected to play a major part in selection. At the same time the players will expect him to be their mouthpiece at meetings and gatherings.

Man-management comes into the job of club captain, especially in relation to selection. It is often difficult for a player who has been dropped to appreciate that he may not be as good as he thinks he is, and the captain has to know how to handle this kind of situation. It is important, for instance, that the man who has been dropped should be the first person to hear about it. The captain must keep everybody informed of what is going on within the club, especially inside the selection committee. Communicating is very important for the success of a club.

The captain must also take an interest in the lower teams in the club, it is not good enough just to look after the affairs of the first fifteen. The other sides in the club must feel that the club captain cares about them and that they are a vital part of the club as a whole. It is also crucial that the captain is present when the teams train. In this way he can not only set an example, he can also get to know everybody and so create a

*The climax of club
rugby in England.
Peter Wheeler, captain
of Leicester, receives
the 1979 John Player
Cup at Twickenham*

*It is important that the
captain sets an example
at training. Here Billy
Beaumont and Roger
Uttley stride out
ahead during an
England training
session followed by
Budge Rogers, chair-
man of the selectors,
Don Gatherer, physio-
therapist, Mike Davis,
coach, and Mike
Slemen*

feeling of well-being and confidence throughout the club. He must keep the interests and welfare of his players at the top of his list of priorities.

One way in which captaining a club side is easier than captaining a representative side is that the players are more familiar with each other's play and with the team's requirements. Roger remembers that when he was captain of Gosforth he could just tell the team to 'step up a gear'. The whole side would then do so, and the points would come.

One good thing about captaincy at club level is that you have probably been in the team for at least two or three seasons and therefore know where your team's strengths and weaknesses lie. You probably know most of the team personally and they know you. The previous season you may have gained ideas as to how your available material could be better used than it was by your predecessor as captain. Now is the opportunity to put your views to the coach, and he will probably let you try them out. Always be humble enough to listen to what other players have to say, especially former captains. Do not necessarily do what they advise, but do them the courtesy of listening to what they have to say and, if you think it is sound advice, act upon it.

Pre-season training can be vital to a successful start to your season as captain. You must set an example by turning up to every session on time and by training as hard as anyone else, if not harder. Work closely with your coach, even if you disagree with some of the things he is saying or doing. It is important for the rest of the players to feel that you and the coach are working in harmony. If you do disagree with the coach argue with him afterwards, not in front of the rest of the players.

If you want to make a rule for the season that a player who does not turn up for training will not play for the team on the Saturday, do so. But do not then make an exception for a gifted player who says he is unable to get to a training session.

52

It is tempting to excuse some talented individual from regular training because you know he will play well anyhow, whether he trains with the team or not, but, for the sake of a happy and wholehearted team, do not make exceptions to your rule. The rest of the team will resent any special treatment accorded to an individual, and it is better to have a happy team without the gifted individual than a disgruntled side with him. If you know in advance that you will have difficulty in getting everyone to attend training regularly — perhaps because the club has a membership drawn from a wide area and travel is difficult — then do not make the rule in the first place.

The captain and coach should jointly work out in advance the programme for each training session, and the coach will then direct the session while the captain takes part with the rest of the team. If, however, the coach wants to deal with some particular aspect of their game with the backs, then the captain, assuming he is a forward, can look after the pack's session. And, of course, if the captain is a back, and the coach wants to work especially closely with the forwards, then the captain can supervise the backs' practice. But remember, training is hard work and it is not easy to motivate players at training sessions, so the captain must be seen to be doing his share of hard work. If the players think the captain is opting out, then they are going to opt out as well. So, as captain, you cannot afford to shirk.

Captaincy can be quite a lonely position. For instance, you will be involved in selection, and there will always be people who are disappointed at being dropped. The captain is the first in the firing line when the complaints come in. Being a captain also means that you should act responsibly not only on the field but off it as well, especially on tour. Neither you nor your team must go overboard and upset people; you can all have fun but you must not be destructive. You must see to it that your team treats other people as they would themselves like to be treated. The captain must be strong enough to say,

'Look, this is not on. Let's calm it down. Let's go and do our own thing in the team-room, not here.' In this type of situation the captain's job is difficult because there will be some strong characters in the party who will turn round and defy you. You have simply got to be strong and firm.

For big matches on big occasions the outlook of the players on the field can depend very much on the motivation achieved by the captain in his team talk before the start. It is possible for a captain to motivate his men to a great degree, but it is worth remembering that it is impossible to do this week after week.

Haranguing will not work for routine club games; it very soon loses its effect when you try to repeat similar methods for what are basically fairly ordinary matches. It is more likely to work with inexperienced players because they are more prepared to accept what the captain says than the old sweats are. But generally, for routine games, the captain will

Peter Wheeler, the Leicester captain, releases the ball under control for his scrum-half

find the essential feature of the team talk is to gather the players together and to remind them once again of all the points you have been going over during the week in preparation for this match. The team talk is really the culmination of the week's preparation during which you will all have taken into account the known strong and weak points of your opponents and will have practised ways of attacking their weaknesses and defending against their strong points. In the team talk you go over once again all the relevant points, summing up what you are hoping to achieve and how you are going to achieve it.

There are, of course, innumerable ways of talking to teams. You may want to end your talk with one of the many clichés, such as 'The talking stops here'. But at some stage you have got

One of the many duties of a captain. J.P.R. Williams, who is a qualified doctor, attends to the medical needs of an opponent

to pick on individuals, and you must remember to deal with them differently according to their differing characters. As Roger says: 'You've got to needle some of them in order to get the best out of them; others just need a word of encouragement. There is a third category too — those who are most like you in the way they think and in their outlook. You can just go and sit with them for a while and talk with them and perhaps ask them if there's anything you've forgotten to deal with.'

Remember that most people's concentration on listening is limited to forty minutes at any one time, so do not make your team talk last too long. The average team talk should not last more than fifteen minutes, provided you have all done your work of preparation for the match during the week. But it is important to get across to the players that a match lasts for eighty minutes and they must have it instilled into them that there is to be no letting up.

The warm-up before the start of the match is as important as the actual team talk. This helps increase the feeling of togetherness. The adrenalin automatically starts flowing because you are aware of the physical situation you are putting yourself into. The period of a few hours before the game can be an awkward time to deal with because the senses are roused by the

56

anticipation of the match. It is important that everyone should relax in this period.

It is vital that, as captain, you should strike up a sensible relationship with referees. There is absolutely no point in antagonising a referee because he is the man who is in control of the game. He should be regarded as part of the game and not as an outsider. You must accept that the referee has a very difficult job to do and you have got to assume that he is doing his best. Even if that best is not as good as you would like, he is in charge and you must accept it.

That does not mean to say that you cannot go up to the referee in the bar afterwards and discuss matters arising from his refereeing of the game. Just as players learn about rugby from talking about the game with other players, so referees want to learn by discussing points not only with other referees but also with the players for whom they have been blowing the whistle. In this kind of post-match discussion referees can improve their refereeing, and players can improve their own game by talking with the referee.

As captain you must come down heavily on any player who shows dissent from the referee's decision on the field of play. The referee may well change to awarding the penalty ten yards nearer your posts, and your player's foolishness may well cost three points. Apart from that, you will be recognised as the head of the team and held responsible initially for the behaviour of your players on the field. Any truculence by your players will jeopardise your own relationship with the referee, and a vital part of the enjoyment of the game will be lost.

It can quite definitely add to everybody's enjoyment of a game if a sensible attitude to the referee is maintained by all. He must not be seen as a man to be deceived or ignored. Some experienced referees may come up to you and say, 'I know what's going on, so just you cut it out', and you do. Or else you, as captain, may say to the referee, 'Look, this is getting stupid, can't we do something about it?' This is the kind of

Captains should strive for a happy relationship with referees. Here Alan Welsby, the English referee, has a word or two with Phil Bennett of Wales and Jean-Pierre Bastiat of France

helpful adult relationship it is possible for the experienced captain to achieve with an experienced referee. It contributes a great deal to the enjoyment of a game if you can keep the lines of communication open in this way.

If your side is penalised for some offence in one of those grey areas of the laws, and you as captain genuinely do not know what the penalty is for, then you are at liberty to ask the referee. But do not go up to him as if you were demanding your rights. Enquire why, do not demand to know.

For those who still will not believe that a captain of a club has to devote a great deal of time to the job, Roger has recalled the routine of a week during his time as captain of Gosforth. He reckons that the club made calls on his time regularly on six days out of seven, the only free day being Wednesday (when there would quite often be something like a county squad session to attend!).

Even Sunday will probably not be free for the club captain. At Gosforth selection committee meetings used to take place on Sunday mornings and would probably last on average about an hour and a half. It was not just a question of picking the first fifteen for the following week's match. There would be reports on how all the club's teams had fared the previous day and suggestions as to which players ought to be promoted from one team to the one above. If the first fifteen had had a disappointing Saturday match, then there would be a long discussion as to what changes in personnel were needed to improve the performance. Were the star players of the second team really ready for promotion to the first? Would they fit in with the kind of play the first fifteen were expecting to have to produce against their next opponents? Decisions had to be taken, and then the players concerned had to be informed.

Monday night at Gosforth was the occasion when the various club committees met to discuss the thousand and one matters which have to be decided behind the scenes for the smooth running of a successful and happy club. At most clubs the

captain is expected to take part in these discussions, and most captains will want to do so because they see their responsibility as reaching far wider than simply the captaining of the club's first fifteen. In this way the captain has an opportunity to help fashion the future of his club, and on these committees he is in a sense the spokesman for the players. The length of time the captain has to devote to such affairs on a Monday night clearly varies according to the number of matters to be discussed and their importance. But a captain can expect his presence to be required for at least two hours.

Tuesday night is training night with the emphasis on fitness. Beforehand the captain will co-operate with the coach in deciding on the content of the training session, and he will try to ensure discipline and get everyone to turn up on time. He, of course, has to set an example in this, as in everything else to

60

do with the club. If the captain shows how keen he is by arriving on time and by training at least as hard as any of the other players, his enthusiasm and efficiency will spread throughout the club. This is also an occasion not to be missed for making and maintaining contact with the players from the other teams as well as the first fifteen.

Unless there was some county or regional squad session to attend, Roger remembers Wednesday at Gosforth as a night off. But some clubs play more or less regularly on Wednesdays as well as Saturdays, and here is further work for the captain to do.

Thursday night is another training night, this time with the emphasis more on tactics. The aim here will be to make use of

Roger Uttley, in his Gosforth days, holds aloft the John Player Cup at Twickenham

whatever knowledge you have of the opponents you have to play on the following Saturday. You have got to plan to expose and exploit your opponents' weaknesses while keeping your own team's weaknesses hidden as far as possible. At the same time you must plan to make the best use of your own team's assets and organise defence against your opponents' known points of strength.

It is no good a club captain fondly imagining he will have a quiet Friday evening with his feet up, relaxing in preparation for Saturday's game. The evening may start like this, but almost invariably there will be telephone calls to be answered concerning players who are crying off at the last moment because of injury or for other reasons. It is the team secretary's job to inform players that they have been promoted to a higher team because of, say, an injury to a man in the team above. But the club captain's advice on such matters will often be needed. And, of course, if a member of the first team withdraws, his withdrawal can have an effect on several teams lower down. If, for example, your first fifteen loses a centre threequarter on the Friday, then the captain has to decide which centre to promote from the second team. And when the second team has had this man promoted to the first fifteen, a replacement has to be found from the third team, and so on down the club.

On the Saturday the captain's job is by no means confined to the eighty minutes of the match. It is not unknown for further changes to be made through players missing trains, going to the wrong ground or having their cars break down. The captain, especially if there have been late changes, has got to make sure that everyone knows and remembers the plan of campaign to be adopted for this particular match. They must all be clear in their minds about the way you intend the game should be played.

After the match the captain has to act as a sort of host to the visiting team, making sure they have as enjoyable an evening at his club as his players would like to have at their opponents' club. This is also a good time to discuss methods of play and developments in the game with your opponents so that you may all improve your rugby. You may also be able to find out something you did not already know about some future opponents of yours. And do not forget the referee and any pressman who may have come to report your match. They, too, want to enjoy their evening, and it will do nothing but good for you, as captain, to establish a happy relationship with both referees and press.

And so, probably very late on Saturday night, the hustle and bustle of a busy week come to an end. . .and then at 11.30 next morning the week's routine starts all over again. But it's worth it.

6 Captaincy at Representative Level

Representative teams are the easiest sides to captain because you are generally playing with a larger percentage of players of a high standard. Basically, the biggest problem is to get everyone thinking along the same lines; it is really a question of organisation, motivation and implementation. If you did not have organisation, you would have fifteen men, each trying to do his own thing.

Roger recalls the occasion he was picked to play for the North-East Counties against the Springboks in the 1969-70 season: 'Phil Carter, who played for Bradford and Yorkshire, was our captain and Rodger Arneil, the Scottish flanker, was pack-leader. Something Rodger said that day really summed up for me what motivation was all about. In his initial address to the pack he simply said "cometh the hour, cometh the man". Now the Springboks were no mean side, and because of demonstrations against apartheid the atmosphere up at Gosforth Greyhound Stadium was electric — no place for a young man of nineteen. But those few words suddenly gave me certainly an awful lot of inspiration on the day.

'Then there were Willie John McBride's words at the team meeting before the 1974 Lions left on the bus for the first Test at Newlands in Cape Town. He simply said "we must go on, there is no escape". We all knew what he was feeling and what he meant, and we went out and won that Test and the series.'

As far as tactics and strategy are concerned the captain in an experienced representative side is the voice of the other fourteen men. They will all have talked together and decided on their plans, and the captain is the man who puts these plans into action on the field through making the decisions. It is all too easy for people to imagine that one man is responsible for the result of a match. The successful side is the amalgam of experienced players accepting on the field the authority of one person in particular but knowing that the decisions this man is taking are virtually theirs because of the discussions held before the match.

In addition to exercising his authority the captain should be big enough to accept the advice of others during the course of a game. Roger acknowledges the help he used to get from Peter Dixon, not only when they were playing for Gosforth but also when they were together in the England team: 'We complemented each other, and I could always ask him to take over the reins for a bit. So many factors are involved that no one person can know all the answers. The captain needs to make use of those about him in the team.

A happy duty for a captain. Phil Bennett, captain of the 1977 Lions, introduces Gordon Brown of Scotland to Prince Charles on the occasion of the match between the Lions and the Barbarians in September 1977 at Twickenham. Fran Cotton (left) and George Burrell (right), manager of the Lions, look on

The mortification of
failure. Alastair Hignell
misses with a kick at
goal for England.
What did his
captain say?

'At the same time the decisions have to be made by the captain himself and he has to accept responsibility if things go wrong. I remember when we were playing for England against France in 1977. Alastair Hignell was having an off-day with his goal-kicking, and one of our plans was a pre-arranged forward penalty move. At this stage of the match we badly needed a score and when a penalty was awarded Nigel Horton screamed for his penalty move. I opted for a kick at goal. The kick missed, and England lost the game.'

There is a temptation at representative level, as at lower levels, to make an outstanding player captain. But this seldom works, unless that player has had plenty of experience. In 1968 Wales picked Gareth Edwards as captain, and at twenty he was the youngest man ever to captain Wales. But in the event his lack of experience proved a handicap, and the selectors switched back to the other end of the age spectrum, nominating John Dawes as captain. Dawes at that time was probably much more worldlywise than Gareth and more experienced in nearly all aspects of life. Experience is vital in a captain.

With the England team in recent years it has been the

J.P.R. Williams captains Wales against England in 1979 and announces his retirement from international rugby

selectors' policy to change the captaincy more often than in other countries. Roger has played under four different captains during his international career: 'In my time I have played under John Pullin, Fran Cotton, Tony Neary and Bill Beaumont, and I have also been captain myself. Some of England's changes in captaincy have been caused by injury, but the underlying message that comes across is that, just as there is no substitute for experience in a player, so the same applies to captaincy.'

While experience is essential in the makeup of a captain, it is not enough by itself. It is no good picking as captain a man of vast experience but who has lost some of his enthusiasm for the game. What matters is to get the blend of enthusiasm and experience right.

Initially, one of the problems of captaining a representative side of any kind — county, inter-district, inter-provincial, international — is that you, as captain, probably do not know your players very well (not as well as you know the players in

The joy of captaincy. A triumphant Billy Beaumont as the final whistle blows in the England v France match of March 1979

your club at any rate) and do not fully know the strengths and weaknesses of your side as a whole. These will become apparent in time, but to start with you will probably have to rely on the advice of your selectors and coach who, presumably, have watched your players often and over a long period. Squad sessions will help you to get to know everyone, and once you get the feel of your side, you can start to influence the way they play. And once you have achieved mutual familiarity your representative rugby can be really well co-ordinated.

One of the best ways for a captain to get to know his players is to go on tour. England's tour of Japan, Fiji and Tonga in May/June 1979 was of great benefit to Billy Beaumont as a captain because it enabled him to have a concentrated period when he was in charge. He got to know everyone and they got to know him, and the relationships forged on that tour probably had quite a bit to do with England's successful championship campaign early in the following year. Similarly Beaumont captained North-West Counties on their tour of South Africa in 1979, and this tour probably had an important bearing on the North's victory over the All Blacks and Lancashire winning the county championship the following season. Lancashire played with the kind of mutual understanding that normally comes only to club sides who train and play together frequently.

Even the 1980 England team had an atmosphere more like that of a club than of a routine representative side. This was partly because most of the rugby the England team played during the period of the internationals was with their fellow England players on account of the short intervals between the international matches and also on account of squad sessions.

7 Captaincy on Tour

Captaining a major touring side is a very demanding job because you are confronted with so many different and taxing situations far away from the field of play. You have to be something of a diplomat in the country you are visiting and you have got to make sure that your men do not go over the top in their social activities. You are in the public eye all the time, and you should set an example and be polite. You have to cope with making and listening to speeches wherever you go, and you may have to cope with the problems of morale associated with a losing side. You have also got to sort out the problems of those players who are not getting enough games for various reasons — they have got to be kept happy. It can all prove too much of a strain unless you have a man of the right temperament and a strong personality.

In all the varied tasks involved with captaining a touring side it is a great help to the captain if he has a frank and happy relationship with both the coach and the manager of the party. In fact harmony within the triumvirate who run a tour can be one of the most vital ingredients for success. The 1971 Lions in New Zealand had as near a perfect combination as you are ever likely to get. Doug Smith, the manager, was a thick-set, tough yet sympathetic man who was always firm and who stood unshakably by the decisions he made. The fact that he was a doctor meant that he was something of a father figure and that the players automatically respected him. They soon learned they would not get away with anything as far as he was concerned. He was content to leave all the playing side of the tour entirely in the hands of his coach, Carwyn James, and the captain, John Dawes.

Carwyn James, perhaps because he had been a teacher, possessed the priceless ability to bring the best out in everybody. He knew instinctively how to approach each individual, and he was humble enough to gather together the views of his players and to form his plans from these.

John Dawes had been a highly successful captain and coach of London Welsh and was respected by everyone in the game. As a trio Smith, James and Dawes were entirely complementary, and Dawes, as captain, had the experience and authority to make vital decisions on the field.

Another particularly well-matched trio was Charlie Saxton, Fred Allen and Brian Lochore who were manager, coach and

The moment of truth for a tour captain. Willie John McBride leads the 1974 Lions into battle in South Africa. Gordon Brown follows him and Sandy Carmichael holds the Lions' mascot which McBride has thrown to him

captain of the 1967 All Blacks in Britain. Saxton and Allen had toured Britain as players with the Kiwis of 1945-46, the New Zealand Services team who did much to revive British rugby immediately after World War II. Saxton, a diminutive scrum-half, captained those Kiwis and Allen, who played first or second five-eighth, went on to captain the All Blacks on their tour of South Africa in 1949. The point is that on their tour of Britain the Kiwis played relentless, open rugby in contrast to the ten-man, tight rugby played by subsequent New Zealand touring sides. So when Saxton and Allen returned to Britain as manager and coach of the 1967 All Blacks, they were determined to get away from ten-man rugby and to brighten the image of their country's game. They were determined to try to win their games by playing fluent fifteen-man rugby, even in bad weather.

The captain, Brian Lochore, as a No.8 forward, may at first have doubted the wisdom of this policy, but he agreed to give it a go, and the triumvirate stood firm against adverse criticism. His All Blacks eventually won fourteen of their fifteen matches, drawing the other one 3-3 against an East Wales side which included Gareth Edwards, Barry John, John Dawes and Gerald Davies. As it happened, the insistence of Lochore that his team would go on playing open rugby probably saved them from defeat in the last match of their tour against the Barbarians at Twickenham. After thirty-nine minutes of the second half the Barbarians were leading 6-3 but Lochore got his men to run from a tapped penalty inside their own half, and their try (worth only three points in those days) made it 6-6. Then, well into injury time, Lochore himself fielded a stray Barbarians' kick and launched an immediate assault which brought the All Blacks the winning try. The point about this tour was that the captain supported the management in their desire to foster fifteen-man rugby, they supported him in his attempts to get his men to play it, and all were rewarded with an unbeaten tour.

It cannot be easy for selectors to pick a captain for a major tour because his job of captaining on a long tour is so different from the normal types of captaincy a player gets involved in at home. A candidate for the captaincy of a major tour does not really get an opportunity to prove whether he could do the job. The selectors can only assess whether he has the experience and at least some of the many qualities required for the exacting task.

The captain of a national side, you might think first of all, is an obvious man to captain a Lions side, for instance. Yet when you think about it this is not necessarily so. The captain of a national side in the international championship is with his side only for short periods at a time over a short campaign. Squad sessions nowadays give the captain at home more chance to influence his players and their combined style of play, but even if he makes a success of leading his country in the championship, this does not mean that he will automatically be capable of inspiring and uplifting a major touring party over a period of two or three months during which they will be constantly living together.

In a sense the captaincy of a club is more akin to captaining a major touring side in that the captaincy lasts for a period of at least eight months. But, again, there will seldom be occasions when the club team are away for days and nights on end, and in any case a club captain can lean heavily, for off-the-field activities, on the various club committees. He is never short of someone prepared to give him advice and guidance.

It is true that a captain on a long tour can, up to a point, lean on the manager and coach. Nevertheless he remains very much the figurehead of the touring party of thirty players. He has not only to be respected by all of them, but he also has to represent them and speak and act for them throughout every day of the tour. He has to be part shop-steward and part ambassador. Those selecting a touring team's captain cannot do much more than look for an experienced captain and then, by getting to know him, decide whether he has the kind of qualities which

will enable him to adapt to the job of captaincy on a long and continuous tour.

The most important quality for a captain of a touring side is a strong personality. He must also have the mental as well as the physical stamina to remain optimistic when things may not be going well. He must be able to lift the twenty-nine other players at the stage of the tour when some members of the party may be homesick and most will be to some degree exhausted. The captain must be courteous to VIPs and bores because the public image of the tour depends largely on the manner in which he conducts himself. It is one of the most exacting positions in sport.

At the same time the captain must maintain his own form on the field so as to be worth his place in the Test team. Willie John McBride was one of the very few who have managed to live up to these demanding criteria. Before he captained the 1974 Lions in South Africa there was never any doubt about his personality and character, but some people doubted his ability to command a place in the Test team on the fast and hard South Africa grounds at the age of thirty-four. In the event he played some of the best rugby of his distinguished career twelve years after the first of his five Lions' tours.

One of the vital ingredients for successful tour captaincy, as for management and coaching, is respect and the best way to gain respect is through sheer natural strength of character and integrity. A tour captain must also be prepared to be punctilious about matters of routine discipline. It is very important, for instance, that he allows no-one to show resentment at the decisions of referees. The captain himself may, and often in a different country with different interpretations of the laws he must, ask the referee for the reasons for some decisions. But the rest of the team must accept the decisions, however unjust they may appear. It never did any side any good to show open dissent about the decisions of a referee. Carwyn James and John Dawes were particularly firm

about this with the 1971 Lions in New Zealand and not only
did they earn the thanks of New Zealand referees, but they also
did much for the image of the tour as a whole. You could go so
far as to say that this attention to detail on the field was one of
the reasons for the success of the 1971 tour.

Off the field, too, the tour captain should ensure punctuality
and that the team try their best to be sociable at the inevitable
and interminable 'after-match functions' and so-called cocktail
parties. The reward for such effort is that every member of the
touring party feels he has contributed something to the image
of the tour. It is not difficult to think of touring sides who have
lost the respect and goodwill of the local rugby public largely
through openly criticising referees on the field and through anti-
social behaviour off it.

The captain of a touring side inevitably has to make a great
many speeches in the course of a tour; the most obvious
occasions are in the evenings after matches. In the British Isles
it is the custom for visiting captains to make formal speeches at
dinners after matches. This is especially true after internationals
which are invariably followed by banquets or dinners at which
hundreds of people are present, some of them distinguished.
At such gatherings there is a formal toast list and both captains
are expected to make speeches. After lesser matches there may
be only a buffet supper, but, again, the captains will be
expected to address the assembled company.

In rugby countries outside the British Isles and France the
habit of holding formal dinners after matches is dying out, even
as far as Tests are concerned. Instead, however, there is bound
to be an 'after-match function' of some kind, usually some sort
of stand-up drinks party accompanied by tit-bits of food such
as legs of fried chicken and meat balls on sticks to be dunked
in soup plates full of tomato ketchup. Invariably at some stage
during these parties the captains will be called upon to speak.
It does not help much that by the time the captains make their
speeches there will probably already have been speeches from

the president of the local union, possibly from the local chairman as well and certainly from the touring team's manager.

Nor is speech-making confined to the two evenings per week after matches. At almost every town visited — normally two towns per week — there will be speeches to be made at receptions laid on by some local body and, in addition, touring captains are much in demand as guest speakers at luncheon clubs. And, of course, players, including the captain, get invited to schools and often end up having to deliver an address to

Moments of relaxation are precious on a long tour. Here some of the 1977 Lions, among them Phil Bennett, Clive Williams, Tony Neary, Gordon Brown, Willie Duggan, Fran Cotton, Andy Irvine and Mike Gibson, watch a Maori war dance

pupils and staff gathered together in the school assembly hall.

It is important on tour that the captain establishes an understanding relationship with the press. It is common practice on tour nowadays for only the manager, coach and captain to be authorised to give official information to the press. This means that the captain is often sought out by journalists eager for something to write about in order to satisfy demanding sports editors.

There is an important difference between the touring press in Britain and the touring press in other rugby countries. In Britain the press living and travelling with the touring party is almost entirely made up of journalists from the visiting country. Thus the regular press corps seldom numbers more than about six or seven. British journalists usually travel to and from each match from their places of employment.

In countries like New Zealand and South Africa, however, several New Zealand or South African journalists usually accompany the touring side for the whole of its tour. Thus the number of journalists making demands on the touring captain in New Zealand or South Africa is generally at least twice as large as it is for a captain touring in Britain.

A captain, apart from when he goes on tour, does not have much need or opportunity to become familiar with the press. One exception to this is the press conference which national captains are now expected to attend immediately after each international in the Five Nations Championship. As with everything else, it takes time to build up a relationship with the press, and it requires experience to be able to deal effectively with journalists.

8 Position

One of the most frequently discussed questions in rugby is what is the best position on the field from which to captain a side, and good cases have been made for every single position. At first sight it would appear that a full-back or wing threequarter is too remote to be able to communicate efficiently with the rest of his team, and it is often said that a front-row forward has to spend too much of his time buried in a group of players to be able to see what is really happening in the broader strategical battle. Yet there have been many successful captains at all levels of the game who have played at full-back or wing threequarter, and Eric Evans, who was England's hooker in the 1950s, is generally considered one of his country's greatest captains, having led England to the Grand Slam, the Triple Crown and the international championship.

The advantage of captaining a side from hooker is that you are right in the heart of the battle most of the time. It is therefore a grand place to lead from by example. The disadvantage, apart from having one's head buried too often, is largely one of communication. The hooker is in ideally close contact with his forwards, but it is not easy for him to keep in touch with the midfield backs, for example. Nevertheless the Lions were captained in New Zealand and Australia in 1950 by Karl Mullen, the Irish hooker, and in 1959 they were again captained in the same countries by an Irish hooker, Ronnie Dawson.

The same advantages and disadvantages apply to having a

prop forward as a captain, and again there have been plenty of successful captains who played at prop. One of the most outstanding was Wilson Whineray who led the 1963-64 All Blacks on their tour of the British Isles and France when they won 32 of their 34 games. He captained New Zealand in 30 of his 32 Tests, and of those 30 matches the All Blacks won 22 and drew three.

Lock forwards, like Willie John McBride and Bill Beaumont, have proved that a team can be well captained from their position on the field. They were essentially men who led by their personal example and by their inspiring dedication and single-minded determination. There is nonetheless a difficulty for a lock in communicating, say, with his centre threequarters because there are not many times in a game when they are likely to be in close contact.

In theory a flanker, because he is part of the pack yet spends much of his time rushing out among the backs, is in an ideal position as far as communications are concerned. But the flanker who plays a loose type of game may often find himself too far from the tighter members of the forwards to give an effective lead to the pack. Two men who have conspicuously succeeded in captaining their teams from the position of roving flanker in recent years are Graham Mourie of New Zealand and Jean-Pierre Rives of France.

The No.8 is extremely conveniently placed for captaining a side. He is very much part of the pack yet he operates in close conjunction with the scrum-half, and the positional options open to him throughout the game demand that he keeps an alert eye on the movements of forwards and backs alike. Mervyn Davies of Wales and Brian Lochore of New Zealand may be mentioned as captains who led their sides with great success from the No.8 position.

As far as captaining a team is concerned the scrum-half is in much the same situation as the No.8. Except when he may be covering deep across the field, the scrum-half is in very close

Graham Mourie, captain of the All Blacks, managed to inspire the whole side from his position on the flank

Jean-Pierre Rives races to score a try against England at the Parc des Princes in 1980. He led the side by personal example and by high principles from flank forward

Mervyn Davies grabs the ball for Wales. He captained his country to great successes from the No. 8 position

contact with the forwards. When he puts the ball into a scrum he can feel exactly how the scrummaging between the two packs is going, and no-one knows better than he what is going right or wrong at the line-out. This is true of the rucks and mauls as well because the scrum-half is in the ideal position to observe the quality of possession being won both by his own team and by the opponents. And, of course, the scrum-half is not only in close touch with the backs as the man who feeds them the ball, but also, having parted with the ball, he is in a fine situation for subsequently observing the relative strengths and weaknesses of the back divisions.

There have been scrum-halves with such personality and voice that they have more or less led the forwards as well as captaining the side. But, generally speaking, if any back is to captain the team, the forwards will need a pack-leader chosen from

82

among them. It is indeed by no means unheard of for a set of forwards to include both a captain and a separate pack-leader. This situation arises either when you have a captain who has a wide knowledge of the game but lacks something of the ability to drive and inspire or when the obvious natural fiery leader of the forwards has not the wisdom or the appreciation to captain the whole side. Ideally, of course, all these qualities should be combined in the one man, but there have been many examples of successful sides in which the duties of decision-making and urging were carried out by two different forwards.

There can be no doubt that if you go as far away from the scrum as fly-half for your choice of captain then you *must* have a forward delegated to lead the pack. And you will seldom, if ever, find a successful team captained by a back who does not owe a great deal to the work of his pack-leader. Provided you have an inspiring and knowledgeable pack-leader, fly-half can be a good position from which to captain a side. At fly-half you are near enough to the forwards to be able to communicate with the pack-leader and you are in close touch with the rest of the backs. You are not near enough to the heat of the forward battle to know exactly what is going on in the engine room but, against this, you have a wider and more constant vision of the game as a whole than can be obtained by those who are nearer in. At fly-half, too, as at scrum-half, you are in an excellent position for dictating the overall pattern of a game.

Most of these advantages and disadvantages apply to centre threequarters as well, the difference being that a centre is a little bit further removed from the forwards and has less opportunity to direct the operations of the side than has the fly-half. But, again, there have been many successful captains who have played in the centre. One obvious one is John Dawes who captained the highly successful London Welsh sides of the late 1960s and early 1970s and who led the 1971 Lions to their triumphs in New Zealand.

A wing threequarter is not quite as much out of touch with

the rest of the team as may appear likely at first sight. When the wing threequarter is right across on the open side he is in contact only with his centre and perhaps with his full-back. But when the wing is on the blind side, he is often in close touch with his forwards and his half-backs, and the same is true while line-outs are taking place on his side of the field. On the whole though, wing threequarter is not an easy position from which to captain a rugby team. That is not to say that there have been no good captains who have played on the wing. Arthur Smith, for instance, captained the 1962 Lions in South Africa from the right-wing, and Gerald Davies seemed to have

84

little difficulty in communicating with his side when he was captain of Cardiff in their centenary season.

A full-back, of course, is even more remote from the centre of activities than a wing threequarter, yet a full-back can give a lead through his courage in defence. The modern full-back has plenty of opportunities to influence the course of a match by joining the threequarters in an attack and by launching himself into counter-attacks. J.P.R. Williams led Wales to the championship and the Triple Crown from the full-back position, and the 1968 Lions in South Africa were captained by Tom Kiernan, the Ireland full-back.

Just as a captain who plays among the backs needs to have a pack-leader to look after the forwards, so does a captain who is a forward require one of his players to lead the backs. And it is important that the captain maintains close and frequent communication with his backs-leader or pack-leader, as the case may be, throughout the game. Ian McGeechan, who played at centre and fly-half for Scotland, was a captain who could make decisions in a detached way and who had a flair for tactical appreciation, but he would be the first to admit that it was vital for his style of captaincy to be complemented by an inspiring pack-leader.

Roger says that, in his experience, he has tended to be involved in sides which were captained by forwards, '. . .and in that situation we have depended mainly on the fly-half to lead the backs. This has not been necessarily because the fly-half has been good at directing the backs, but rather because in his position he has been handily placed to convey information from the captain in the pack to the rest of the backs. It's really all a question of communication.

'Ideally there should have been such thorough communication before the match between all the players that each of the fifteen men should know what his individual role is and what are the roles of the other fourteen at any given moment in the eighty minutes of a game. In such an ideal world you would really not need a captain. But you can never quite achieve that perfection. Therefore captains and pack-leaders and leaders of the backs all have important jobs to do.

'As a matter of fact the 1980 England team had so much experience and had played and practised together so much that we all knew what we were doing and we had really reached the stage where the role of captain is less important. Where Billy Beaumont was so valuable to the side was in the inspirational effect of his example.'

9 Famous Captains

Captains tend to be judged by the measure of success their teams achieve. But, while it is probably true that a successful team will nearly always be found to have a good captain, it does not follow that every unsuccessful team has a bad captain. If you think of the Lions teams over the years no-one is likely to deny that John Dawes, who captained the successful 1971 Lions in New Zealand, and Willie John McBride, who led the

John Dawes, captain of the 1971 Lions in New Zealand, leads Wales onto the field for the match against England that year

successful 1974 Lions in South Africa, were good captains. On the other hand, this does not mean that, for instance, Tom Kiernan, the Irish full-back who led the 1968 Lions in South Africa, or Ronnie Dawson, captain of the 1959 Lions in New Zealand, were bad captains.

Going back to the 1971 Lions' tour of New Zealand in which the Lions triumphed in the Test series, the fact that New Zealand were beaten in that series does not mean that their leader, Colin Meads, was a bad captain. On the contrary, he seemed to make a good job of captaining a none too well equipped side. Among New Zealanders we have tended to think of Wilson Whineray, who was in charge of the 1963-64 All

88

Colin Meads

Blacks in Britain, and Brian Lochore, who led the All Blacks on their visit in 1967, as being great captains. Undoubtedly they were very good indeed, but they were at the same time fortunate to have in their parties so many men of rich experience who knew what to do and who did not need much motivating. Men like Ken Gray, Denis Young, Colin Meads, Kel Tremain and Waka Nathan scarcely needed to be urged. The more experienced a player is, the more he can produce fire from within himself.

Such players do not need — and do not like — the tub-thumping, ranting and raving type of captain, they prefer a more sober, more mature type of leadership. That is not to say there is no place for the loud, inspirational style of captaincy. Eric Evans, generally regarded as one of England's best captains having led them to great success in the 1950s, was said to invoke the spirit of Dunkirk at the drop of a hat. The point here is that the England side he started with was not an experienced one and his forceful, extroverted type of leadership was what was needed to bring the best out of his young team.

Evans, of course, built up his side at a time when there were no such events as squad sessions. But there were three trials each season before the first international, and Evans used these as a means of welding his team together. In fact he started by captaining the junior side and eventually carried almost all his junior forwards with him into the England team. If you talk to any of those forwards they will tell you that the leadership of Evans was very largely responsible for getting them their first caps.

The most suitable style of captaincy depends not just on the amount of experience in the team but also on the particular national temperament. The French, for instance, seldom play well unless they have a man of strong personality to lead them. The classic example of this was when Lucian Mias, the lock forward, led them to victory in their two-match Test series against the Springboks in South Africa in 1958. That was the

Four captains in the van. Willie John McBride leads the pursuit of the ball followed by Fergus Slattery of Ireland and by Tony Neary (right) and England's John Pullin

first tour the French had ever made to a leading rugby country and, after drawing the first Test 3-3, they won the second 9-5 at Ellis Park, Johannesburg. The irony was that Mias was not in fact captain of that French touring team. The official captain was Michel Celaya, the man who has since had a spell as coach to the French national side and who still looks after France B, but he was hurt early on that tour, and it was Mias who took over the captaincy for the two Tests.

Mias was a jovial extrovert whose personality made him a born leader. When France went to play in Dublin in 1959, there were rumours of illness sweeping through the side on the Friday evening. When the French players came down to breakfast in their Dublin hotel on the Saturday morning, they found Mias sitting in an armchair at the bottom of the stairs, apparently counting heads. When eventually Alfred Roques, the vast, bald prop who played his first game of rugby at the age of twenty-six and won the first of his twenty-eight caps at the age of

thirty-three, came waddling down the stairs, Mias stood up and addressed him: 'Alfred, I'm sorry, but today you must play scrum-half'. With all the rumours of sickness flying around, Roques was probably not quite sure whether his captain was joking or not. But, such is the authority of Mias, you got the impression Roques would gladly try his hand at scrum-half if it would help his captain.

Then, more recently, there was that tough, little scrum-half, Jacques Fouroux, a tiny man with a hideously lobbed pass who was technically not a very good player. But Fouroux had a Napoleonic personality which made him not only respected but

92

almost worshipped by the rest of his team. Throughout his career he had a running battle with the outspoken French rugby press who reckoned he was not worth his place in the national team. Fouroux had the last word by leading France to only the second Grand Slam they had ever achieved, in 1977.

Another Grand Slam man, Graham Mourie of the All Blacks, must be rated as one of the best captains for his feat of leading a none too talented side to victory over each of the four home countries on the All Blacks tour of 1978. It has often been stated that none of the home countries had really good sides that season, yet the fact remains that no previous All Blacks side had ever managed to beat all four home countries on one tour. It was also often said that those All Blacks were not really a very good side, so all the more credit to Mourie for leading them to those triumphs.

10 Great Captains

WILLIE JOHN McBRIDE

Roger reckons Willie John McBride the best captain he has come across in all his long experience of rugby. 'He had the most presence of any of them, both on and off the field,' says Roger. 'On the field he was a competent rather than brilliant player, but as captain of the 1974 Lions in South Africa he was absolutely superb. He was particularly good at giving confidence to the less experienced members of the party. Somehow he had an almost fatherly attitude to the young players.'

One of his great moments came before the team left the Arthurs Seat Hotel in Cape Town for the first Test on that 1974 tour. About twenty minutes before the bus was due to leave the hotel, the players assembled with their kit bags and moved into the team-room. They found McBride already there, sitting alone with his pipe in his hand. Nobody said anything. The players just trouped in quietly and sat down in silence. McBride likewise said nothing until it was time to leave for the Test at Newlands. 'Right now, let's get up and go,' was all he said then, and they all went out to the bus resolved to do great battle for him that day.

McBride was also given a unique distinction during the Lions' tour of New Zealand in 1971. He was made captain for one match even though the tour captain, John Dawes, was playing in that game. What made this gesture on the part of the Lions' management all the more remarkable was that McBride at that stage of his career had never even captained Ireland, let alone the Lions. Moreover four men who had already captained their

Willie John McBride, captain of the 1974 Lions, is chaired off the field at Port Elizabeth by Gordon Brown and Bobby Windsor and led away by Ian McLauchlan after the Lions had made it 3-0 in the Test series by winning the third Test 26-9

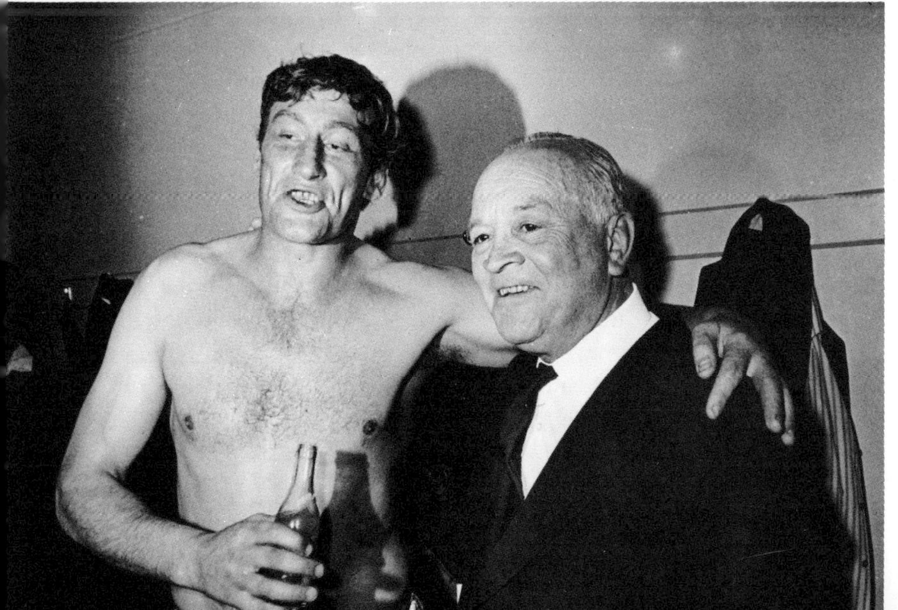

Captain Willie John McBride is congratulated in the dressing room by Danie Craven, president of the South African Rugby Board, after the Lions had won the third Test at Port Elizabeth

countries — John Dawes of Wales, Mike Gibson of Ireland, Frank Laidlaw of Scotland and Bob Hiller of England — willingly played under McBride that day at Palmerston North.

That was the fourth of McBride's record-breaking five Lions' tours. He had started in South Africa in 1962 and had then gone to New Zealand and Australia in 1966 and to South Africa in 1968. He had forced his way into the Test teams of 1962 and 1966, and he had become an automatic choice as Test lock in 1968 and 1971. By 1971 he had become the Lions' pack-leader, and this day at Palmerston North against the combined side of Manawatu and Horowhenua he had his first taste of captaincy. He gave what we later came to know as a typical McBride performance, leading by his vigorous personal example and refusing to allow his team to relax even when well in the lead. The Lions won the match 39-6, and John Dawes and Frank Laidlaw carried McBride shoulder high from the field.

Then there was McBride's famous remark on the Sunday following the Lions' victory in the first Test on that 1971 tour at Dunedin. On the Sunday morning the Lions had flown to Queenstown, a place beautifully situated at the head of a lake, for a couple of days of relaxation. While there they all gathered in front of a television set to watch the film of their exploits of the previous day — all, that is, except McBride. Just as the programme was about to start, in strolled McBride with a glass in one hand and his pipe in the other. He ambled across the room, leant on the television cabinet and looked at his fellow Lions. 'Come on now, lads,' he said, 'What would you be wanting to look at that for. That's all history now.' And, with that, he moved off into the other room to sip his drink and suck his pipe.

McBride was as steady as a rock. No-one could be more vigorous and determined than he on the field. But he also knew how to relax. His inspiration on the field came from his example and his very presence. As Roger recalls: 'If Willie John said "Come on, boys, we've got to raise it," everybody did.'

MERVYN DAVIES

Mervyn Davies won thirty-eight caps for Wales between 1969 and 1976 as a No.8 forward, and until his illness in 1976 he was expected to captain the 1977 Lions in New Zealand. He played in all four Tests for the 1971 Lions in New Zealand and in all four in South Africa in 1974. Roger remembers him as 'A wonderful No.8. He always struck me as being "the elastic man". He was a bit of a beanpole, but he always seemed to be able to stretch further than anyone else. As a captain he won respect because of his sheer ability on the field, while his close understanding with his scrum-half, Gareth Edwards, gave confidence to the rest of the side. He was much respected off the field as well because he could drink and smoke with the best of them. He was a tremendous No.8 and a shrewd tactician.'

Mervyn Davies, No.8 and captain of Wales, ready to pounce on a loose ball

PHIL BENNETT

Phil Bennett captained Llanelli, Wales and the 1977 Lions in New Zealand, and perhaps his greatest asset as a captain was his exceptional ability to score points. His kicking was especially useful on the 1974 Lions' tour of South Africa when he did a lot of damage to the Springboks. His kicking could do wonders for his side. He had a side-step that could win a game, and the sudden and dramatic effect he could have on a game, either kicking or side-stepping, used to lift his team's morale. He had a similar effect on his teams with his ability to find his way out at moments when he appeared to be under severe pressure.

In his days as captain of Llanelli he was greatly helped by the presence of such players as Derek Quinnell, Ray Gravell, Roy Bergiers and J.J. Williams, and they all helped him to mature as a captain. In the Welsh national side he could count on help from everyone. He was not an out-going man, so this support and help was vital to his successful captaincy.

Phil Bennett, captain of Wales and of the 1977 Lions in New Zealand

BILLY BEAUMONT

His outstanding season as captain was the 1979-80 season when he first led the North of England to their famous victory over the All Blacks at Otley, next captained Lancashire to the county championship, then took England to the international championship, the Triple Crown and the Grand Slam, and finally was chosen to captain the 1980 Lions in South Africa. He was fortunate to be able to develop his captaincy with such strong sides as Lancashire and the North, and he matured as a captain on England's tour of Japan, Fiji and Tonga in May/June 1979. On the field his greatest asset is the way he can lead by personal example.

The 1980 Lions will not be known as a successful side because the record books show that they were defeated 3—1 in their Test series against the Springboks. But, in spite of these defeats combined with an unprecedented list of serious injuries and in spite of political pressures, they remained an extra-ordinarily happy touring party. Billy Beaumont must take much of the credit for uplifting his men and maintaining their morale throughout the tour.

Billy Beaumont is chaired off the field at Murrayfield after England had beaten Scotland to win the 1980 Championship and the Grand Slam

JOHN PULLIN

John Pullin, who won forty-two caps between 1966 and 1976, had the unique distinction of captaining England to victory over South Africa at Ellis Park, Johannesburg in 1972 and then the following year leading them to victory over the All Blacks at Eden Park, Auckland. He was the first captain Roger played under for England, and Roger says he was 'always very quiet but a good bloke and one that all the players had a lot of time and respect for. He was a tremendous hooker, and everybody respected him for his ability there. He was quite a shrewd captain and good at raising morale and keeping the side plugging away.'

In spite of his quiet manner, he always made excellent speeches at dinners, humorous and witty. One of his nicest remarks was made at the dinner after Ireland had beaten England at Lansdowne Road. This was the season following the one in which, because of the Irish troubles, both Wales and Scotland had declined to travel to Dublin. 'We may not win all our matches,' said Pullin, 'but at least we turn up.'

John Pullin, captain of England and a fine handler as well as an expert hooker, runs with the ball against France accompanied by Peter Dixon

IAN McLAUCHLAN

Ian McLauchlan, captain of Scotland but playing here for the 1974 Lions in South Africa, goes down for the ball, closely supported by his Lions captain, Willie John McBride

Ian McLauchlan was a highly skilled loose-head prop on the Lions' tours of New Zealand in 1971 and South Africa in 1974, and he made his mark as captain of Scotland. He was a hard captain, calling a spade a spade and not pulling any metaphorical punches. He was always very deeply involved in the game, and was much respected because of his experience and his reputation. He had a good grasp of the game and was a sound tactician. He was an excellent tourist and a very likeable person off the field. Experienced men are essential on any tour, and McLauchlan was one of the senior props on the 1974 Lions' tour of South Africa, giving the tour management a lot of assistance.

Ian McLauchlan, as captain of Scotland, watches closely as Alastair McHarg picks up the ball against Wales

ANDY LESLIE AND GRAHAM MOURIE

Andy Leslie and Graham Mourie have both captained the All Blacks from the loose forward positions, Leslie being captain against England in New Zealand in 1973 as well as on the All Blacks' Irish Centenary trip to the British Isles, and Mourie captaining them in Britain in 1978, 1979 and 1980. Roger, who played against them both, considers them very similar players and expert readers of a game. 'Of all the captains we have spoken about in this book, these two were the most tactically aware I have come across,' he says. 'When England were in New Zealand in 1973 they wheeled us about and messed us up dreadfully. Mourie probably had the edge over Leslie in pace about the field, but they were really very similar players and tremendous captains. Mourie was a wonderful leader by example and a very strong disciplinarian on his tours here, mainly because of the example he set.'

Andy Leslie, one of New Zealand's cleverest captains

Graham Mourie, captain of the All Blacks, sums up the situation

IAN McGEECHAN

Ian McGeechan, captain of Scotland, was talented enough to play either at centre threequarter or at fly-half at the highest level of the game. He played in all four Tests on the Lions' tour of South Africa in 1974 and again in all four on the 1977 tour of New Zealand. As captain of Scotland he brought a lot of flair to the Scottish team. He was not the kind of man who cared for the limelight, but his modesty did not prevent him from gaining great respect from his team-mates and from his opponents. He was a very shrewd tactician.

Ian McGeechan, a shrewd captain of Scotland and a clever midfield back for the 1974 and 1977 Lions

FERGUS SLATTERY

Fergus Slattery, a flanker with the 1971 Lions in New Zealand and the 1974 Lions in South Africa, has been a fiery motivator of Irish teams in conjunction with Noel Murphy, the Irish and Lions coach. Roger describes him as 'the original ball of fire. Perpetual motion on the field. In his younger days he was as quick as most backs. He is a very intense person on the field with a favourite trick of yelling at opposing fly-halves as he runs at them. A tremendous personality and a great shouter of Irish ballads. His main attribute as a captain is his motivation. He is a very positive person and a great character. He lives life twenty-four hours a day whereas some people can manage only about twelve.'

Fergus Slattery, captain of Ireland against England at Twickenham in 1980, seems to be shouting as he watches Billy Beaumont, England's captain, pass the ball to the English scrum-half, Steve Smith, near the Irish posts

JEAN-PIERRE RIVES

Probably the greatest achievement of Jean-Pierre Rives, the blond French flanker, was to lead France to victory (24-19) over the All Blacks at Eden Park, Auckland on 14 July (Bastille Day) 1979. The French scored four tries that day, just a week after the All Blacks had hammered them 23-9 at Christchurch.

But Rives did much more than that. When he took over the captaincy from Jean-Pierre Bastiat he broadened the forward-dominated game the French had been relying on. He was subsequently unlucky with injuries to key players and other problems behind the scenes, but he refused to compromise with his own very high beliefs and standards, and he had to take a lot of stick for the stand he had taken. He was not prepared to sit back and let things happen. It takes courage to do what he has done because you run the risk of having someone come along and stick a knife in your back. He stood up and said what he thought should happen, and in doing this he earned great respect from his own team and from the opponents of France.

*Jean-Pierre Rives,
courageous captain of
France*

PETER DIXON

Peter Dixon had won only one cap, against the President's Overseas XV during England centenary celebrations in the 1970-71 season, when he played as a loose forward in three Tests for the 1971 Lions against the All Blacks in New Zealand. He went on to win twenty-two caps between then and 1978 and was a most intelligent footballer. Yet he was discarded after only the briefest reign as England captain.

Dixon captained England at an unfortunate period. As Roger says, 'A captain needs things to go right for him. You've got to keep clear of injury yourself, and the key men in your side have got to stay clear of injury too.'

Roger never played for England under Dixon, but he knew his captaincy well at Gosforth. 'He was not the easiest person to get to know,' says Roger, 'and some people called him a loner. This was perhaps his biggest problem as a captain at representative level, but he was very good company both on and off the field. He is an anthropologist, but we never held that against him. In fact we called him 'Lennie'. He was always prepared to stand up and be counted. Of the captains in my experience he was probably the greatest tactician of the lot.'

Peter Dixon, one of the cleverest of captains, looks for his support